WORLD-BUILDING SPACE OPERA

Business for Breakfast: Volume 15

BLAZE WARD

Knotted Road Press

Also by Blaze Ward

The Handsome Rob Gigs

Can't Shoot Straight Gang

Can't Shoot Straight Gang Returns

Hunting Handsome Rob

Handsome Rob, Assassin

The Jessica Keller Chronicles

Auberon

Queen of the Pirates

Last of the Immortals

Goddess of War

Flight of the Blackbird

The Red Admiral

St. Legier

Winterhome

Petron

CS-405

Queen Anne's Revenge

Packmule

Persephone

Additional Alexandria Station Stories

Siren

Two Bottles of Wine with a War God

The Story Road

The Science Officer Series
The Science Officer
The Mind Field
The Gilded Cage
The Pleasure Dome
The Doomsday Vault
The Last Flagship
The Hammerfield Gambit
The Hammerfield Payoff
The Bryce Connection

Shadow of the Dominion
Longshot Hypothesis
Hard Bargain
Outermost
Dominion-427
Phoenix
Princess Rualoh

Hunter Bureau
Mirrors
Latency

World-Building Space Opera
Business for Breakfast: Volume 15
Blaze Ward
Copyright © 2021 Blaze Ward
All rights reserved
Published by Knotted Road Press
www.KnottedRoadPress.com

ISBN: 978-1-64470-197-3

Cover and interior design copyright © 2021 Knotted Road Press

Reviews
It's true. Reviews help. Even a short one, such as, "Loved it!" So please consider reviewing this book (and all of the ones you've read) on your favorite retailer site.

Never miss a release!
If you'd like to be notified of new releases, sign up for my newsletter.

http://www.blazeward.com/newsletter/

Buy More!
Did you know that you can buy directly from my website?

https://www.blazeward.com/shop/

This book is licensed for your personal enjoyment only. All rights reserved. This is a work of fiction. All characters and events portrayed in this book are fictional, and any resemblance to real people or incidents is purely coincidental. This book, or parts thereof, may not be reproduced in any form without permission.

Thanks for extremely useful cogent and useful comments go to Ken W. Burnside

1

A Public Thank You

I NORMALLY WRITE these Business for Breakfast books as almost streams of conscious captured on paper. Then the Fabulous Publisher Babe™ reads it, makes a few comments and corrections, and we publish. However, since this was not a topic she's all that familiar with, I reached out to a few people with deep love and understanding of World-building for Space Opera, and asked them to review the initial draft.

I am deeply indebted to Ken Burnside of Ad Astra Games (https://www.adastragames.com/) for reading the draft and adding some serious commentary and expansion in places. Most of the math is his, so blame him for anything egregious and blame me for copy/paste errors where I might have screwed it up.

He made this a better book by also brain-dumping, as well as refining my initial thoughts. Simple as that.

I first met Ken at the 2016 WorldCon in Kansas City, when I got invited to lunch with Daniel Keys Moran and his lovely wife, Amy. Ken ended up randomly next to me and we nerded out down at that end of the table. I have stayed in touch with him since, because the man is smart. Here's a slightly modified bio I stole from the interwebs to help frame him for the rest of you:

Ken Burnside is the designer of Attack Vector: Tactical, Squadron Strike! and Saganami Island Tactical Simulator. He runs Ad Astra Games and made a cameo appearance in Mass Effect 2 alongside Winchell Chung.

Ken was nominated for a **Hugo Award** *in the* **Best Related Work** *category for his non-fiction article "The Hot Equations: Thermodynamics and Military SF."* (Ed. Note: No award was given at Spokane in this category after the Sad Puppies Debacle.) *"The Hot Equations" puts several assumptions about the future of space combat under a microscope, using reasonable extrapolations of technology and accepting fundamental laws of physics. While aimed at hard SF authors, the article is equally applicable to designers working on hard science fiction games.*

You can find a copy of "The Hot Equations," at Ad Astra Games.

You should go look up The Hot Equations and probably get yourself a copy if you want your hard SF to be nerdy and correct in those sorts of things.

Thanks, Ken.

And now on with the show.

2

B4B: Space Opera

Author's Note

I'M SORT OF BEING BLACKMAILED. Fabulous Publisher Babe™ wanted to take a drive to think about what her next novel should be. She's been writing serious stuff and wanted something…not frivolous, but totally out of her normal range of things.

Originally, she wanted to take a long drive. That's what we do when we want to deep dive some writing/publishing topic. As we were watering the plants tonight, space stories came up and she latched onto writing some space-based SF.

We're not talking Hard SF here. Many people think of that genre as the science fiction where someone requires all the tech to be "realistic." But that isn't really science fiction. It's just adventure fiction and I find frequently find it boring as hell because writers often focus on getting every little scientific detail correct, at the cost of taking the time to write a good story. I want bigger stories than whether or not we can land a spacecraft on the moon. Been there. Done that. So last Thursday.

I like grand stuff. So I started rattling off ideas and questions to her about how I world-build when I build a new SF universe. It's August 2020. She took a SF Workshop in the Dark Ages of January 2020, and got a solid grounding then, but has been largely writing mystery and epic fantasy for the last six months.

But as I'm talking, she looks at me and says "You need to write all this down as a B4B, because other people want to know and don't know who to ask."

Okay, then. Consider yourselves warned. This is not an academic study. It is how I happen to work.

At this moment, I have the following Space Opera universes (complete, in process, being published, or with at least one full novel done): Alexandria Station (Jessica, Javier, Handsome Rob, Doyle, Henri, Suvi); The Dominion (*Longshot Hypothesis*, et al); Star Dragon; Star Tribes (*Winterstar*, et al); Lazarus of Bethany (2021); Taft Station; Kincaide (*The Eden Package*, et al); *Fairchild*; and a whole host of shorter collections of things not yet published, including the Brouson Dynasty that my Patreon supporters know. All of those are different. Completely. Not reskinned retellings, but completely new starting points working outwards.

So, yeah, maybe I can talk about the topic. With that in mind, let's talk World-building your Space Opera.

Some Working Definitions

First and foremost, what are we talking about when we say world-building? For me, it has a specific meaning, because my undergraduate majors were Political Science (Military and Global Power) and Philosophy (Epistemology or the Study of Knowledge). Plus, I minored in Social and Urban Geography, which is a nice way of saying I have a map fetish.

World-building, then, talks about a whole host of things. What is the primary political structure of the main place people will hang out? Democracy? Republic? Tyranny? Oligarchy? Timocracy? Theocracy? That makes a big difference, because the leaders have different wants and needs and that shapes what they do to the universe around them. What about other places your heroes might visit? Good trouble requires massive differences of opinion.

Similarly, what is your economy based on? Slave labor? Guilds? Unions? Unfettered Capitalism? Command of the Industrial Heights? Socialism? Again, that creates all sorts of issues and gaps.

Without going too deep here, you will need to do more than just take the United States, slap a new coat of paint on it, and call it good. I mean, sure, some people don't want to think, but they wouldn't be reading science fiction in that case.

Good science fiction posits "What if...?" and then explores it in a story. With your world-building, who did you base it on? A lot of folks have commented on Jessica Keller by saying "well, when I was in the Navy..." (meaning US Navy, circa 1980-2010, ballpark), to which I ask what their Command Centurion thought about that and watch them sputter. I didn't base Aquitaine's Navy on the US, but on early Imperial Rome (First and Second Century CE, and even then only loosely).

Study history and find things that make you wonder. And laugh out loud. **Everything** has been tried somewhere.

Writing Styles

Are you an architect or a gardener? I dislike the terminology of plotters versus pantsers, because usually it is used dismissively by people who spent months carefully crafting a plot in an outline, then transferring that to note cards and color-coding them, before editing and rearranging and getting everything just so.

I watched a woman do such a thing on her social media feed, and tracked her. She started her outlining work on the same day I started a novel. I finished my novel, writing into the darkness, before she finished her note cards. I finished the novel *after that* by the time she started writing her opening paragraph, which then took her two weeks because it had to be crafted just so. She spent the better part of a year on a seventy thousand world novel. I spent a little over a fortnight.

I write fast. She would rather walk the same hundred miles six times with extensive redrafting, while I've walked six hundred miles. But I am also a good enough writer that I can let backbrain/writerbrain just tell a story and it will be good.

How?

Lester Dent. The Seven Point Plot Structure. I wrote another B4B on the topic: *The Beginning Professional Storyteller*. Note, not Professional Writer. I am not a writer. I am a storyteller. I can write compelling things into darkness because there are certain rules.

Find a **Character**; in a **Setting**; with a **Problem**; go.

In Science fiction, setting is *EVERYTHING*. You can handwave Modern. The word 'Western' conjures a backdrop in your head. As does 1930s Private Eye. But in Science Fiction, you're going somewhere new, so you have to ground the reader hard in the setting and do so early.

That means details. Not just description, by the way, but how does the Character FEEL about what they see? Does it remind them of happy summers at grandma's house making cookies? Does it remind them of being shipped off to that crazy old woman in the country every summer when they were a kid? Same event, different feelings.

I am a gardener. I plant seeds and then garden around them as they grow up. Some of you are as feral as I am. Others of you are architects, feeling better about getting every little detail on paper, each chapter, each everything, before you start.

This is how I work; do what works for you and don't argue with me here.

EXERCISE

Are you an architect or a gardener? Understand that it might change with every project, but you need to know that going in, especially as this entire book should be thought of as a massive checklist for you to consider.

SO, have I riled you up and started your juices bubbling?
    Good, let's go.

3

Chapter: Space Opera versus Space Adventure

FOR ME, the first question when spinning up a new universe is Opera versus Adventure. That is: What is my scale?

Space Opera is a huge thing, where the fate of the entire galaxy might be on the line. In the original trilogy of Star Wars Movies (Star Wars, Empire Strikes Back, Return of the Jedi), we were all about overthrowing an Evil Empire™ and restoring the benevolent Republic. (It's right there in the name: The Alliance for the Restoration of the Republic or "Rebel Alliance.")

So then, huge fleets, huge problems. Huge story.

As someone pointed out when reading the first draft here (KW Burnside, Ad Astra Games):

> *"Big stakes imply big agency on the part of the protagonist. Star Trek is Space Adventure Stories, Star Wars is Space Opera.*
>
> *It is much easier to make episodic adventures in the former, and much easier to tell stories about moral conflicts in the latter; space opera has*

more in common with epic fantasy than a noir thriller.

Space adventure can be that noir thriller (the Expanse) or a philosophical rumination on the nature of punishment and what to do with an escaped war criminal in a civilized society (Star Trek's The Conscience of the King)."

When writing space opera, you have to make sure that the stakes go up with every single novel. (Or movie.) The story arc from *Auberon* to *Petron* for Jessica Keller shows that. By the end, we've overthrown a god and are threatening to set an entire octant of space on fire in a massive war that might bring down all the civilization we've come to know.

Big stakes. Escalating crises. Problems bigger with every step.

On the flip side of things, you have what I refer to as space adventure. The key here is that the stakes are both smaller at the start, and don't have to get bigger each time. My own example is the Shadow of the Dominion books, starting with *Longshot Hypothesis*. Valentinian is just trying to make a buck, but he gets pulled into someone else's problem and has to find a way to thread the needle between legal and ethical so that everyone comes out ahead.

That's book one. Book two starts with a poker game where our hero wins a treasure map. Lemme tell you, when I set out to write this series, that game was just supposed to be the first part of book two, but it took over and demanded an entire novel unto itself, so the series went from five novels to six. But books two through six are all about that damned treasure map. Other things happen, with the Widow and such, but they don't any of them threaten to spill over into galactic civil war.

I've gotten reviews from people complaining about Glaxu

and how little supposedly happens in books three and four, but that's because those are stories that involve side characters advancing the overall plot, which is still Dave versus the ex-wife he abandoned. Eventually, we have the big running gunfight that takes up a novel and a half, but you gotta lay all the ground work.

EXERCISE

So, first question for you as you start world-building: Opera or Adventure? How big are your envisioned stakes?

Additionally, how black and white is the morality in your universe? This is where *Setting* blends into the *Problem*. Space Opera is a typically a morality play of some sort; we want the villainess to twirl her mustachios, casually commit war crimes, and for the heroine's forthright goodness to make them worth cheering for, and for that goodness to **matter** in the end.

Mere grandiosity of made-up politics does not a Space Opera make. You need heroes and villains.

The downside of this is an understanding that Space Opera deals rather poorly with nuance. Things must be black and white at some level, so if you wish to gray things around you end up spending a lot of time adding details and exposition that tends to slow your pacing considerably.

You don't have to know your actual problem at this point (Character, Setting, **Problem**) because these are all *Setting* questions, but the bigger your problem, the bigger (deeper) your world-building will have to be in order to cover it. The more details you need to get down ahead of time, which leads me to the next point.

4

Chapter: Write It All Down or: "I Can't Be Wrong"

THIS IS a big thing in SF, and you will hear from armchair historians who think you got it wrong. I can't be wrong when I write science fiction. I can only be inconsistent.

Read that again.

I cannot be wrong, I can only be inconsistent.

If the ship has four powerspears paired in dorsal and ventral turrets in book one, it damned sure better be the same in book three. Or you have to have a refit somewhere that changes it. A certain subset of your fans will lock on those details and throw a fit. And write you hate mail.

From one of my topic experts (KW Burnside, Ad Astra Games):

> *If you're one of those writers who came to this racket from gaming, statting out your ship/alien/whoseamawatsis in a gaming product is worth your time early in the process rather than later. It gives you consistency to work from.*
> [Blaze: I did exactly that when building all the vessels I used in the

Jessica Keller universe. Specifically, I actually did SSD sheets (logically drawn from my days of playing the original Star Fleet Battles by Amarillo Design Bureau) for every class, regardless of whose side they were one. (Some of you might even recognize the Andromedans in later books.)]

After talking to one of my gamer designer friends in writing this, he pointed out that nothing, and I do mean nothing, is more sigh-inducing than having a game company go through and canvass your work to discover that your superdreadnoughts are the density of cigar smoke, or that you've had a ship grow and shrink and grow again with each book.

Games (board, card, or computer) have different constraints and different world-building requirements than a series of novels do. Specifically, they demand more numerical rigor, and there are more things you can't do in them than when you're spreading words on the manuscript page.

Those limits can lead you to interesting stories, however.

One kind of gaming-induced limit that should be eyed with trepidation is

> *travel times and logistics. (And we'll circle round to this again later.) These are very real concerns for real admirals and generals and political agents, but they should show up as complications rather than walls of exposition the reader has to slog through.*

Plan ahead and think about your technology with some rigor and detail, and do so at the top.

I once got a review once explaining how I had gotten the physics of my space drives all wrong in one of the Jessica novels. This was impressive because I have NEVER to this day bothered to figure out how they work myself. Reviewer had just assumed he knew how it worked and had to correct me. I almost wrote to ask him how they worked, but figured that would be rude.

In the Lazarus books, I actually talk about how the Light Starcruiser *Ajax* flies on gravitational waves rather than propellant, because that becomes a significant plot point in two places. (Mostly when the alien asked why they don't sneak up on someone, then fly away backwards shooting at him. A *Kaufman Retrograde* for some of you and a *Parthian Shot* for the historians in the audience.)

What does this all mean?

If you plan on writing a big space adventure or opera series, you need to start taking notes even before you start writing words. For me, when I am ruminating on a new project, I open a "Notes" doc file and dump ideas into it. Characters, Settings, Problems, the works. Anything. Everything.

In the Jessica Keller Books, every character **who has ever gotten named** has an entry. If there is a description, it gets copy/pasted so I have it forever. Fashion. Looks. Personality. All of it.

Similarly, every ship. Every planet. Everything.

I cannot be wrong, but I can be inconsistent by not getting

all my details correct across novels. By the end of *Petron*, you've seen that description of her black, regal outfit four times, because I pasted it out of my notes and then tweaked it each time. Just enough that you have to be paying attention, but same enough that you recognize it.

There are people who dislike keeping an encyclopedia as they start writing multi-novel space operas. Those people are fools or dilettantes—take your pick—because then they have to go back when they finish the book and pull all those details out by hand, inevitably missing something. Worse, they might have to hire someone else to build it for them, at a huge cost of time and money.

Editing slows everything down if you don't, because I promise you will not have remembered the details correctly, so now you have a First Reader asking what color her eyes really are, because they were blue here and green there. (Jessica's are green. I have had to look that up enough times to remember it even today.)

Big Space Opera is the kind of thing that spans 250,000-1,000,000 words. Lots of novels, side stories, prequels, sequels. *STUFF*. You need to write down all that Setting beforehand or at least as you go. You will never get it all sorted out later.

NAMES

For me, I go a step beyond everything listed above in my prep. I use a couple of random generator programs and use those to spit out alien sounding names, as well as SF kinds of names: http://donjon.bin.sh/scifi/name/

If you look on the left side of the screen, you'll see a metric shit-ton of other available generators, but I stay on this page and generally use the alien names option for both people as well as planets/stars. Sometimes the fantasy name generator gets called on as well. The option for Planet Names lower on the drop-down has a decided American/English flavor to it, which can be good in some places, but find that it works against me when doing most things.

You will also see a drop-down option for Starship Names. That's actually where "Longshot Hypothesis" came from. I hit it generating for a different project, but loved that name so much that I added it to a brand new notes file that eventually became Dave and Valentinian, but only much later. Again, a very Human/Earth flavor to ship naming, but that can be beneficial or detrimental.

The point I want to make is that you can quickly generate 30-50 names for aliens, species, or planets from a single list, add them to the Notes doc, and then just pull things out as you need something on the fly later.

Remember: I write into the dark, or at least dimly-lit hallways, so I might know I will need a few alien species (Lazarus of Bethany used bunches), and it saves me time. For you architects, it can also move you out of a place where all your people and all your aliens have similar names. Random works much better to get people in the flow.

On the flip side, I have another trick for naming Humans in an Earth-based universe (more on the meaning "Earth-based" later.)

I start with an online dice generator like this one: https://www.wizards.com/dnd/dice/dice.htm

The bottom row lets me put in a d63. (63-sided dice. Wonderful invention.)

I roll two d63 and remember the results before going here: http://www.behindthename.com/random/

Three columns of twenty-one names each, or sixty-three options. I have fun by generating two numbers, selecting the appropriate cultures, and then running with it. Corynthe, in the Jessica Keller books, came up with Japanese and Scottish. Yeah, I had fun with that.

Next, back to the dice roller for a d4.

If I don't care who my walk-on character is, I let the system randomly select gender options, where the drop-down choices are Masculine, Feminine, Ambiguous, or Either.

Random Surname: check.

Generate a few until you find one that really jumps out at you. I usually have first, middle, and last names, and frequently will open the results in new tab so I can see what the various names actually mean. Again, lots of fun and some of those combinations immediately suggest personality notes to me, helping me round out a person who will appear for one scene and leave.

This is, by the way, something that many early role-playing used so many random tables to spark the imagination.

The **Traveller** Roleplaying game is particularly useful this way for making random worlds, because when people need to come up with them from their own brains, they have about four:

A) Ancient Planet of Mysterious Horror

B) Planet of Extreme Environment {Desert, Glaciers, Jungle, Ocean Storms}

C) Planet of Future City of Plot Dispensing

D) Place We Sell Stuff At And Never Leave The Starport.

It is more fun to let the system randomly spit things out if it isn't plot-critical. Plus (and we will dig into this later), there is no such thing as a single-culture or single-environment world and you need to think about that.

Another trick I have heard suggested is to turn those die tables into decks of cards, and make a tableau ala Tarot, for designing some of your walk-on characters and even worlds. Again, the key is to add some real randomness to things and not just have every NPC be a cardboard cutout who walks on for one wooden line and then leaves.

Or, in the case of a certain tailor, ends up taking over a novel and writing himself into all subsequent books as well. But that's the Vibol magic.

[NOTE from my other reader:

When selecting alien names, please remember to make the

main characters' names pronounceable. You will drive readers away if they can't actually say any of the names they're reading about. Or you can make the primary name unpronounceable, but then give them an easy to remember nickname.

One trick that I use is to use dojon, from up above, and I select a culture other than the standard English/British, such as Babylonian or Sumerian. Then I generate all the names for that particular species using that culture. That way, a reader intuitively knows that an individual is from X species just based on the name.]

EXERCISE

Gardeners: Go generate you a couple of lists of crazy, random shit and let those inspire you to make some people. Maybe add some characters.

Architects: Think about the interface between two or more cultures, and how each sees the other, including at least two things they take as ground truths about the other that are misperceptions or flat out prejudices.

Grab a list of names for each culture, and then swap two names each – these were places started by one culture and assimilated by the other in the past.

Cultures and languages mix. Languages also drift. A few inexplicable things that your characters accept as truths lends a lot of depth to your work with very few words on your part.

5

Chapter: The Box

THIS WAS the one that actually locked Fabulous Publisher Babe™ into what we were doing and where she said I should write all this down. I call it **The Box**.

After you have decided the scale of your story universe, and started writing things down, you have a set of decisions to make that will sort it out for you.

	Earth Based
No Aliens	
	Aliens
Non-Earth Based	

Fig 1. The Box

As you can see, we have four options, from answering two

questions. First: Will there be aliens in your universe or not? In the Alexandria Station universe (Jessica, Javier, Suvi, et al), I consciously chose not to have aliens. (Yes, I realize that Doyle messes things up, but I don't consider that story canon anymore, and they were all Human originally, so it still doesn't count.)

One side note on the box before we get too deep is to think about the primary government your characters will deal/fight with. Lots of little interplanetary governments competing and dealing tends to be better for Space Adventure type stories, while a "Big Monolithic Empire" is usually a good starting point for your Space Operas.

If you have aliens, they need to be alien (see later chapter). Or you need a reason that they are all just Humans with a cheap nasal prosthetic. And you'll need to explain it at some point. Your reason can be silly, but you need a reason. Most space pulp from the early days presumed that humans would emerge on all worlds, but that was mostly so they could take old sailing stories from the South Pacific and add space ships. Thinly veiled chauvinism and racism, as it were. Plus, exotic alien princesses with all the appropriate plumbing for our lantern-jawed heroes to seduce.

Will your aliens be more advanced technologically, less, or the same? As the old joke goes, "In space, if you find them, they are in trouble. If they find you, you're in trouble." Build your alien culture up. Make sure that unless your aliens are quite weird, that there will be multiple alien sub-cultures present, even within a given space-faring species. Just as there's no such thing as "Human culture," US Americans exploring space from the 1960s would go about it radically differently than US Americans exploring space from the 2020s, let alone Hindus from South Asia or Maori with star drives. (Personally, I need someone to write me that latter. Sounds like a lot of fun, but I don't have the background knowledge to do it justice.)

Also, ask yourself how the aliens entertain themselves. What is their equivalent of the 'Stock Western Story?' The single hero rising up to challenge the villain (a la Campbell) is a very Western European thing. Other cultural heritages can give you a useful template that occasionally make you think: "Hey, that's odd" which can in turn lead to interesting stories.

Okay, on to the second part of the grid. Will your universe be Earth-centered or not? Star Trek, as an example, is Earth-based, while Star Wars is not. It really doesn't matter that much, but it alters your flavor of things. In the Lazarus books I am almost done with, I invented the Galumph, a six-legged herbivore about the size of a rabbit, and filling the same ecological niche on worlds in Innruld Space. Will a non-Earth-based universe have wolves or whales? You can use the terms, but you'll need to pay attention. And maybe invent Galumphs instead, as long as you describe them well enough.

From The Grid, you start with four radically different kinds of universes and the stories you can tell. In the Brouson Dynasty stories (Brannon), there are no aliens, but Human culture has been in space for at least thirty-five thousand years. Earth is a myth. Brannon, when she is exploring, is finding worlds where Humans lived at one time, but moved on or died out maybe ten thousand years ago. It is an uncommon direction to world-build, but that's what writer brain wanted.

A NOTE ON AI

A lot of folks love Suvi.

She's the *Sentient* computer system that was Javier Aritza's ship in *The Science Officer* series. I made a point of making her as Human as possible for an electronic life form, but she is still an alien, technically. The only alien lifeform in that universe, and an uncommon one, because when Humans started allowing AI's to be warships and planetary factories, the machines created a problem. They didn't rebel, so much as started pursuing their own wars and vendettas, and Humanity was collateral damage as both sides decided to start bombarding worlds in order to destroy factories and economies.

If you include true AI, you will need to deal with them as aliens. Data, in Star Trek: Next Generation, had several story lines where he explored what it meant to be Human. Suvi wants the same, but she doesn't have a body until much later. Instead, she has a consciousness matrix that can be moved around. Eventually, she gets an android body that is close enough to fool humans to the touch, but she will live forever, so she can't stay in one place more than a few decades.

And mind you, when she meets Jessica, she is a little over six thousand years old. (6015, because I have a spreadsheet tracking all those things. See previous chapter on writing everything down.) I have plans for a new round of Suvi stories set starting in 15,006 CE, when she will be nearly 7,600 years old.

Extremely long-lived species like Suvi will have a different approach to things than one only living a century or two. I just finished an epic book one (Kincaide) where one species lives 6,000-8,000 years as a rule. Their ruling House has been on the throne longer than Humans have been a distinct species.

Pay attention to those sorts of things. Can an AI live forever, if their hardware can be routinely replaced? Suvi's future stories actually revolve around that, because the Alexandria Station universe will crash again, and she won't have the parts she needs, so she will have to do something about it.

EXERCISE

Pick each of the four options from The Grid and envision what your Space Opera universe will look like. Identify a movie or television series that embodies each of the four and think about how you could have done it better.

6

Chapter: Measuring Things

ANOTHER INTERESTING AND fun question you'll need to think about when you start world-building is what measuring system you will use. I'll assume that (having written this book in English) most of my audience is Anglo-American. The rest of you will understand and appreciate shortly.

The United States of America uses a so-called Standard System, also occasionally called Imperial, since we inherited it from the British. Weight is measured in ounces and pounds. Distance in inches, feet, yards, furlongs, and miles. Temperature is normally described in Fahrenheit.

Normal, yes?

Except that the rest of the world generally uses the Metric System instead. A German reader might not know what five-foot-seven means as a height without first doing some math. (1 inch = 2.54cm, so 5'7 is just about 170cm tall.)

When I start a new universe, one of the first entries I put at the top of my notes document is Imperial or Metric measurements, to remind me. And I use both about evenly, at least when writing future SF. For Modern and 20th Century stuff I tend to keep it Imperial, because in the US that is the standard.

But what will we use in space? I have long presumed that

Imperial will only survive for perhaps the rest of my lifetime, and then everyone will be on the Metric system. Technically, Richard Nixon ordered us there in the early 1970s, but it never took.

The British and later the Americans were both, in their times, world-dominating imperial powers, so they could do whatever they wanted, and everyone else had to make adjustments. The United Kingdom might not even last all that much longer as a political entity, and the US has already peaked and is facing the Decline and Fall of the [Roman] American Empire in our near future.

So when you build your future culture, do you use Imperial or Metric? If they are British or Americans translated forward, like so much of modern, Western science fiction already is, then it makes sense that those people would do things the old way. Additionally, American readers will understand feet and miles and pounds, while non-Americans need to stop and translate.

You should also think about your aliens, as well as your non-planetary human cultures (born and live entirely in zero-g space without returning to "standard gravity"). What would they use to measure normal distances, and how will you explain it to your readers?

While it's unlikely we will return to the Chinese Imperial *Li* as a unit of measurement barring a civilizational collapse and resurgence, nearly every human culture has a unit of ground distance that roughly equates to "about twenty times the convenient distance to walk to the market."

Time is another place to get a little nerdy. In the Outcasts of Heaven Belt, and in Growing Up Weightless, both authors measure time in kiloseconds. If your culture doesn't live on Earth or doesn't live on planets, look at alternate timekeeping systems.

But be careful in doing this this. It's easy to overuse and confuse your reader. The last thing you want is them stepping out of the story to do math. They might not come back.

World-Building Space Opera

SIDEBAR: Speed in Hard SF/Solar System Stories

A friend of mine who writes a lot of nonfiction makes a convincing case that the unit of human-centric velocity measurement in space is the kilometer per second (km/sec). 1 km/sec is 3,600 km/hour, or 2,237 miles per hour.

One km/sec is near enough to Mach 3 as to make no difference. A *very high power* rifle round's muzzle velocity is about 1 km/sec. The main gun of an M1A2 Abrams tank has a muzzle velocity somewhere between 1.8 and 2 km/sec.

One km/sec is puttering-along-speeds for orbital transfers; it takes about 7.25 to 7.5 km/sec velocity to reach Low Earth Orbit (LEO). It takes 11.6 km/sec to escape the Earth/Moon system, or about 4 km/sec once you're in LEO.

If you're willing to deadhead on a Hohmann transfer orbit, going from Earth to Mars is about 3.5 km/sec.

Delta V is measured in km/sec, as is (as shown above) orbital transfer velocity requirements. While I don't recommend calculating delta v requirements for every story, having a good frame of reference for what you can do with different amounts is useful – my friend suggests this:

15-20 km/sec: Inner solar system travel, fuel is a concern, you don't do course diversions.

21-70 km/sec: Enough delta-v that you can start doing 'tramp freighter in the solar system" stories, going out to Saturn.

70-150 km/sec: Tramp freighter stories out to Neptune, and Edge of the Unknown stories out to the Kuiper Belt.

150-500 km/sec: Plausible fly-by probes to nearby stars. At 300, you can do colony ships in the scale of multi-decade trips.

500+ km/sec: At this point, you're using *magic space drives.*

Keeping it Straight

I frequently take a utopian approach to my far-term, earth-based space opera. (I write grittier stuff that assumes a global apocalypse of some sort in the near future, but that's not this book.) I try to use Metric for those Utopian stories. Especially my new EuroWest Science Authority stories with Cornelius Langa. Those are Solarpunk, set a few centuries in the future, where I marry the EU with Africa as a single political/social/economic entity facing off against the Anglo-American Alliance. (Barbarians, by then. First story is in Boundary Shock Quarterly #13: Solarpunk.)

So let's talk conversion.

I cheat. Flat out simple as that. I have created a spreadsheet with tabs for every scale I need to convert back and forth, so I get my numbers right the first time. 1 inch = 2.54 centimeters. 1 mile is approximately 1.6 kilometers. Water boils at 212F and 100C. 1 kilogram = 2.20462 pounds, but I can round to 2.2 and call it good.

I also took the US Census data from 2010 and dropped every unique first name (5500) and last name (90,000) and built a randomizer that will generate me a name if I need it. For the Lazarus series, I pulled out two thousand "Hispanic" names from another website so I could use them for that series and have them all handy without repetition.

What this does is let me think in Imperial, which I mostly still do because that's what surrounds me all the time, and convert to metric cleanly. Vo Arlo is listed in my notes as 6'8 (2.0m), and 275 lb / 125k so that I have things as I need them. 6'8 275# is a big man. American football player big. But I have to stop and think about 2m and 125k. Easier to write it all down.

Similarly, I list temperatures where twenty degrees is a nice day. But that's 68F.

My Canadian fans are familiar with having to deal with Americanisms and converting in their head. Similarly, my German fans who can read English are probably familiar enough. But that means that you and I have get those numbers correct up front. (One of my copyeditors is Canadian. I just assume she's right when she corrects me there, but I'd rather not make her correct me at all.)

On the flip side of things, I took to heart a forward David Drake frequently includes in his science fiction, where he talks about how the measurements we use today will be archaic and unknown in some distant future, where they will have their own systems. However, he's dealing with modern readers, so he doesn't ever feel the need to invent radically-weird systems that he has to then explain. If you make the reader stop and do math in the middle of the story, you might lose them. Don't give them any chance to escape.

You should not go to all that work, unless there is some story-critical element involved (and your ego on the topic is not story-critical. Tolkien bores me to tears because he introduces so many things that make the world deeper; but detract from the story itself to the point I can't read it.)

Decide up front if you will use Imperial or Metric. Be consistent across the whole series, but you can change your mind for other series. I have a post-apoc series where Persian mechanics routinely bitch because their stolen American hardware is frequently Japanese, so they end up having to carry two sets of wrenches to fix things.

Distances, heights, weights, and temperatures should be "invisible" in the story, much like writing "he said" is. Convey your information and don't make the reader work.

And have fun from there.

7

Chapter: The Drive System

SO ACCORDING to Einstein and a bunch of hard-core, nanny purists, **Faster-Than-Light** (FTL) travel in any form is impossible. Hard Science Fiction, then, as they see it, cannot leave this solar system in anything less than slow generational ships or giant colony ships somehow filled with popsicles that they will thaw out when they arrive somewhere. Along the way might might also use robots to terraform whatever planet they find. Those can be useful stories to tell, but I'm not really into science fiction Space Opera that so limits itself.

Nor should you be.

Instead, let's talk about various drive systems that can get you to the stars and what implications they have for your worldbuilding.

First off, as we mentioned above, the **Not-As-Fast-As-Light (NAFAL)** drive, where you are sailing between stars at a slow speed. A friend recently calculated that we could get a ship from Earth to Alpha Centauri at more or less current technology, in something like 20-30 years depending, assuming acceleration, turnover, and deceleration at the far end to find a place to land. And that cost was not prohibitive to the project.

These are going to (probably) be enormous ships. One

option includes creating the population of a colony beforehand, and then sending it. This means that everyone has to pay attention to who can breed with whom, in order to keep a good genetic diversity going. They'll live aboard some sort of ark that will carry them to their new home, but it might take lifetimes to get there, allowing for problems where maybe something goes wrong with the ship and they need to fix it or be doomed. Maybe they have been flying so long that they have forgotten they are aboard a ship? (A common enough trope when I was a kid reading these stories.)

Next up is the classical **Warp Drive** that you might be familiar with from some of your old television shows. It was much more common in the way old days. E. E. 'Doc' Smith used it a variety of ways, hand-waving that Einstein had either been wrong, or that scientists had found ways around such limitations. The ship is sailing through real space, but doing do somehow faster than light-speed, such that they are like a maritime ship on water. You can get there quickly enough, but time passes.

Not running into something at trans-light speeds is something of an issue, but you can generally get around that by presuming that you are either warping a bubble of space around yourself, or collapsing space in front of you so that you sail a shorter distance, thereby sweeping away all the rubble and debris that might be hidden in the darkness. Whatever, as long as it sounds good and you keep it consistent.

Engaging in combat at trans-light speed is problematical, as beam weapons would be "too slow" to be effective. You might use missiles that can somehow also exceed light speed. In the Star Fleet Battles universe (licensed from Star Trek: TOS but not a 1:1 map), they use warp engines to get between worlds, and then turn around and also fight each other at trans-light speeds with various beams and torpedoes that move trans-light.

This leads us to perhaps another box, depending on how

nerdy you need to be and how important combat between ships will be. Space Opera is all about it, while Adventure less so.

Create yourself another box like you did before, but we'll call this one the FTL Box.

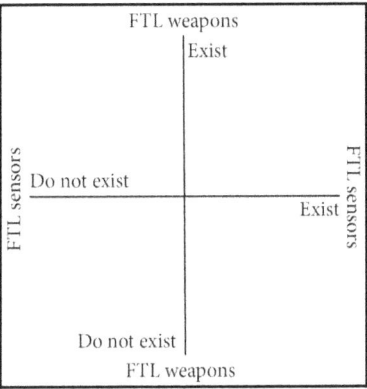

Fig 2. The FTL Box

This will lead you perhaps to some very interesting places where your technological limitations can be baked right into a story that might not work any other way.

To get around space and speed limitations, some writers use a **Hyperdrive** system. The ship just simple opens a portal and goes wherever it wants, but does so in something of its own, personal universe, where it won't run into any other ships. Or maybe it might be able to detect someone in "other space" and you can have piracy and such over there, where a ship might disappear forever.

One advantage of hyperspace is that a small ship might just be able to fly from point A to point B without worrying about anything or anyone in between, if you don't want to spend a lot of time *Walking To Mordor*. This lets you the storyteller focus your narrative on what happens at your interesting worlds you come up with.

On the flip side, the question for Hyperspace is how fast a

ship can transit. In Star Wars, depending on which retcon of the technology Lucas was using at the time (and there have been several), it might be instantaneous to get between places, or it might take a few days or even a month to go a long distance. They were never consistent, depending on the story they wanted to tell (screen or book). (They did not write it and down and stick to it. But they needed to be cinematicly exciting.)

I used the logic of a slow-to-medium-speed hyperspace in the Alexandria Station universe, where they go to Jumpspace and then navigate around stars as they get to their destination, but move with something roughly like the speed of sailing ships, so that crossing great distances might take great time.

In the (currently-upcoming) Lazarus of Bethany books, the Rio Alliance has a technology where they open a portal between two points and instantly step through, with a flash of blueshift or redshift respectively announcing what just happened. I make travel take time for them because they have to aim a vector, jump, land, look around, and maybe jump again maneuvering around stars and gravity wells like Javier Aritza does in the Science Officer stories. This is the opposite of being able to step perfect from the orbits of Caladan to Arakis, as Herbert does in the Dune books.

With Hyperdrives, there is no right or wrong answer. Only consistency, so feel free to make something up, but then stop and think about how that technology impacts on a variety of things that might in turn alter how you tell a story.

How are communications handled at the speed you move? Can information get somewhere instantly, or does it have to be carried on a ship between systems? How quickly can a warrant for your arrest be received from someplace, anyway? Is there an ansible (a device that is functionally a galaxy-wide telephone system so you can call anyone)?

This also impacts trade, and how materials get from point to point. It is pretty easy for a full-developed planet to become largely self-sufficient in things, but when you are just starting out as a colony, are you mining ore and importing food? Farming and then trading for industrial goods? Are you a factory that does nothing else and has to import thing? How quickly can you get stuff from here to there? I have used the storyline of loading up large ore carriers and flying them through hyperspace, rather than taking the time to put smelters and refineries close to the materials. There were reasons. But in the other situations, pirates are going to be looking at valuable goods routinely going from Point A to B and maybe they want to intervene.

Finally, how is warfare are impacted by the amount of time it takes to get there from here? We can fire missiles that drop nuclear weapons on any city in next to no time, but in 1982, the United Kingdom had to assemble and sail and entire war fleet to the South Atlantic after the Argentine government invaded the islands the British call Falklands. A lot of mischief took place during that time, and more could have. How long until the posse gets here?

Next on the list is the concept of a **JumpGate**. This is a fixed point in space, usually related to a station who can generate such a thing as a (semi-)permanent hole in space. Those turn FTL travel into something more like riding a train or an airplane, depending on how long it takes to get there, just as hyperspatial travel does. If you want fun, you can also have the JumpGate open onto some sort of permanent subway system connecting various planets, so again, we have to spend time getting from here to there. Or maybe we have to catch a train to B. Then take another one to C. Finally, we catch a local to D. As you can see, lots of options for things to go wrong when you have to change planes/trains. Missed connections. Lost luggage. Whatever.

Lastly, let's talk (extremely briefly) about **Relativistic Speeds**. This is where you accelerate a ship close to light speed and send it across the cosmos. According to Einstein, the closer you get, the more relativism comes into play. For the crew of the ship, perhaps a month or a year passes, inside the relativistic bubble of their ship. Meanwhile, outside the ship, years or centuries are passing.

For the crew, they will age at a different speed than everyone else, so that friends and family left behind will grow old and die while they are in motion. If they are to return, civilizations might fall and be replaced. Think the original Planet of the Apes movie with Charlton Heston (1968), where they return to an unrecognizable Earth more than two thousand years later.

The travel between stars is a big chunk of what makes Space Opera and Space Adventure so much fun for me. But there are implications.

LAW ENFORCEMENT

How do the cops chase down and catch the bag guys? If you have personal hyperdrive systems (your ship can go anywhere by itself), then probably you and your bad guys can escape any jurisdiction. At that point, your heroes just have to outrun the cops to a certain point and they are free, rather like how US county sheriffs in the early part of the 20th Century didn't have radios to call for help, and didn't have hot pursuit agreements with their neighbors, so as soon as anyone crossed the county line they could pull over and smile at you safely from beyond legal reach.

A lot of law enforcement is thus likely to be defensive, catching bad guys when they return to civilization. Alternatively, if you have a space piracy problem, you can equip a hidden warship to hunt them when they come after you.

All of this, of course, presumes that FTL communications do not exist (see your FTL Box above), and that information can only flow at the speed of whatever ship carries it. Things are very different if your magic or technology includes something like an Ansible (mentioned briefly above). Ursula K. Le Guin coined the word "ansible" in her 1966 novel Rocannon's World as a tool that allows near-instantaneous communications over galactic distances. As such, you can talk in almost real time with someone under a different star, like you were on the phone or perhaps texting them.

Whatever you choose, the implications to governing and the law will be profound, and you should spend some time thinking about it.

EXERCISE

Identify your favorite movie, book, or television series based on the type of FTL they use. Why does it appeal to you? How might you use similar logic? What would you change/fix if you were using the exact same technology to get around?

8

Chapter: Gritty versus Idealized

I LIKE to think of this as the classical Star Wars vs. Star Trek debate. These are broad strokes, so don't take anything too personal or serious, but think about the two series in grand scale.

Before George Lucas, space was usually seen as a bright, clean, cheery place, filled with able, adventurous men and women, usually in silly costumes that involved a lot of silver lamé. Think disco before disco, as it were.

With Star Wars, you got a universe reflecting poverty and aging. Old ships that broke down a lot. Wretched hives of scum and villainy. ***Jawas.***

Now, flip this back just about a decade, to the original run of *Star Trek: The Original Series*. That was a vision of the future that believed in progress, where want and need could be conquered if we kept on this path. As someone suggested when reading a rough draft: "Star Trek: TOS is two parts Swiftian Morality Play to one part Horatio Hornblower In The Kennedy Administration." I'm not likely to argue with him, either.

By the time you get to Star Trek: The Next Generation we might even call it Full-bore Utopianism.

There was little money in the conventional sense because we

all lived in a socialist/communist paradise where it was "from each according to his ability, to each according to his need." (Also, how do you create money that can't just be counterfeited in a Replicator, anyway?) When the ships got to a place with racism, or maybe overpopulation, those were presented as backwards, barbaric places that could be educated into the bright future of the United Federation of Planets, but only after they had developed enough that the Prime Directive was no longer needed.

As you world-build, how greasy, dirty, smelling, or old is it going to be? I like to flash back to the thought of Steampunk as a genre, in an era where people maybe bathed weekly. Maybe. Daily bathing was sinful and wrong, until much later, so people would wear the same clothes, with the same funk, for long stretches of time. (That always gets left out of the books, somehow.)

I imagine that the NCC-1701 Enterprise smelled like a field of lilacs and feral roses in spring, regardless of the condition or day. On the flip side, the Millennium Falcon was usually grease, ozone, and whatever they had for dinner, nine days in ten. (What do you suppose wet wookie smells like, anyway?)

How often will your ship break down, just getting from A to B? What stories will you tell about accidental discoveries along the way? When you walk into a bar, is it a space western? Scum AND villainy? Or Miss Kitty and the Long Branch Saloon?

This sort of thing extends outwards in all directions. The Empire of Star Wars is itself a clean, sharp, military place, with somber, muted colors. Contrast this to the Rebel Alliance, which was at once colorful and mismatched, reflecting a group of hard-scrabble punks fighting the most powerful military organization in the galaxy.

The Enterprise of Jim Kirk and Jean-Luc Picard was always bright and clean, especially on comparison to either set of Klingons. Again, a visual difference that would come down to smells if you were to walk those decks.

Frequently, that level of bright cleanliness is a reflection of money. Of an economy that has enough spare change to repaint the walls every year. To repair every little thing as soon as it happens. The grittiness is often reflective of a ship and crew just barely hanging on. The captain is only making enough cash to keep the life support systems and engines running. You'll eat whatever past-their-expiration-date food he could scrounge, or bring your own. Hope y'all like oatmeal for breakfast every morning. (Firefly fans in the audience?)

However, maybe the oatmeal you're eating just to survive on your ship happens to be one of the most dangerous narcotics on some world, because of what it does to the mind chemistry of some alien. In my Lazarus novels, there are drugs being smuggled around that do terrible things to the overlord species, and pretty much nothing to all the other aliens out there.

Money equals culture equals money

For a non-SF scale of comparison, consider that the 1950s in the United States represented something of an economic peak that will likely never be attained again by this culture. From there, inflation and depressions set in and everything got worse economically in many ways (even as it slowly got better socially), leading to the stagnation of the 1960s, the stagflation of the 70s, and the rampant inflation ever since, as living standards have slipped and continue to fall.

Or as William Gibson once told us: "The future is already here, it's just distributed unevenly."

EXERCISE

In 1955, a white husband could work full time, and earn enough to take several weeks' vacation, get a new car every year or two, and have a wife who stayed home as a full-time homemaker for a brood of bright, energetic kids. Think about those old cartoons, and compare them to the gritty nastiness of cyberpunk or some of the darker movies and series you know.

How will you explore the gritty vs. idealized view in your world-building? What does it do to your story, if the same character came from an Upper Class household instead of a Lower Class one?

9

Chapter: Technology and Toys

A FUN EXERCISE is going back fifty or eighty-five years and look at how they envisioned technology in the future. Not a lot of folks had smart phones, although Star Trek did create a device that actually inspired a lot of folks who later invented such toys. Similarly, there are monetary rewards today as people create modern interpretations of the old tricorders. Writing in the early 1970s Niven and Pournelle even had a device that was all of a smart phone except the camera/video, but neither of those men, I'm given to understand, imagined the impact an actual smart phone would have on everyone.

As you build out your grand technology and civilization, think about consumer electronics, and how they will work. Will there be a world-wide-web that you can connect to when you arrive on a planet? Instant phone calls anywhere on the globe, with only the light-speed lag as you talk to satellites and maybe nearby moons? Ansibles?

Or will your government crack down on such things and only allow certain information? *1984* the book and *Brazil* the movie both explore dark, bleak futures where information is strictly controlled.

How will information be transmitted? Princess Leia put a

disk in an astromech droid that had the complete technical specs of a battlestation the size of a small moon. That's a lot of Petabytes of stuff, I'm guessing.

Will the characters listen to music? I don't remember many movies where music or headphones were featured, but how many people that you know are constantly immersed in the tunes with cords or things stuck in their ears?

Will your space opera have cyberware? Datajacks where you can connect your brain directly to a global or ship-wide network and instantly get information, videos, news, and whatever else? Will a Heads-Up-Display inside your eyes be the successor to the smart phone?

Now, consider the dark side of that tech. I don't want a modal Rickroll in my head that I can't turn off. (Bonus points if that previous sentence actually made sense to you without looking the words up.) Do you? How do you protect your silicon against bad things and bad people?

When world-building a new universe, I usually create an entire chapter called "Technology" and then just dump things in there as I name/use them.

Smart phone, handheld, handcomm, DataPortal. These are all names I have used for that particular piece of gear.

Tablet, slab, Datascreen. The bigger version that doesn't fit in your pocket, assuming we aren't to the point where we can fold it up and tuck it in a pocket.

Here's another one that hit me while I was soaking in the tub last night, thinking about old movies. In this "modern" technological age that you have joined me in, there's one bit of kit that nobody seemed to think of in the old days, when visualizing the future.

How many of you have a padcard ID with a chip built in, either on a lanyard or hooked to a retracting string on your belt? You use that to get into secured buildings and to keep unwelcome and disreputable people out. I had to deal with that both on my job and as a vendor at a variety of places. Or even a basic keyfob that are now used in modern apartments and automobiles

So how do you secure your physical perimeter on a daily basis, without guards actually patrolling around? What happens when someone loses one? How hard are they to hack/spoof?

How do you keep people out? Or in?

Think of all the normal consumer electronics you take for granted right now. Are they available in your SF future? What form do they take?

WEAPONS

In Space Opera, some sort of personal combat is likely as part and parcel of the morality play aspect of it. You are likely to need a pistol-like weapon held in one hand. Star Trek TOS had hand phasers. Star Wars had blasters. Wherever you go, you will need a gun.

I presume that in a distant future, chemically-propelled slug-throwers like a Colt .45 or a .44 Magnum revolver will be archaic and not carried. Heavy. Noisy. Small ammunition magazine. Recoil in a zero-g environment will send you ass over tea kettle. Perhaps a way to signal grittiness where the heroes have exciting beam weapons and the disreputable folk have to rely on guns instead?

However, in really hard SF, it's kinda difficult to come up with something that works as well and as cheaply!

What will replace them if you do?

Maybe electromagnets firing tiny quills like needles? Not really damaging, unless they are made of some sort of chemical that causes someone to keel over unconscious or maybe poisoned. You could do a larger version that rail-gunned a slug. Or scale that up to a rifle that might be powerful enough to blow a hole in a 20th century tank.

Phasers are really just complicated lasers. Blasters are supposed to fire a small packet of plasma inside a magnetic envelope, hitting the target with both heat and kinetic energy. Both are really just things designed for the screen, moving slow enough that the audience can track them, rather than light speed.

Lensman Kinnison had his DeLaMeter pistols, the most powerful beam weapons around, because he was a big, bad, manly type of dude, much like Dirty Harry had his Ruger. Luke Skywalker and Ben Kenobi both carried laser swords that could cut through damned near anything given time. Han had his BlasTech Industries DL-44 heavy blaster pistol that is almost as famous as he is.

What weapon might need to become a signature thing for your main characters? Swords are not the thing for Space Opera, until you can use them to deflect blaster bolts. Warhammer 40k uses chainswords. (Think chainsaw blade on a sword. Seriously.)

Firearms are generally loud, because the slug is supersonic, but if your target it ray-shielded, he might laugh your blaster off. Paul Atreides used a personal shield that would stop anything moving quickly, so you had to fight using the slow blade.

Protection

You should also think about defensive technologies. America's current, ongoing sets of wars have casualty rates that would be deemed utterly miraculous and science-fictional to a commander even as recently as Vietnam, to say nothing of the World Wars, because troops going out into firefights wear body armor that will stop rifle rounds, routinely. This is, of course, causing the US Army to spend money on developing rifles that can get through body armor as well as prosthetics for limbs that are lost to a wound that would have been fatal even a generation ago.

It's possible to get bulletproof tee shirts today that will stop most low velocity pistol rounds at something longer than short range. You'll have cracked ribs and a hell of a bruise, but that bullet won't go into your internal organs and kill you.

World-Building Space Opera

Historically, body armor fell out of favor as first crossbows and later muskets could penetrate it. The first pieces of body armor that got removed covered the legs; they were uncomfortable and slowed the wearer down if they had to walk more than a quarter mile or so. The breastplate was still "strongly advised" as armor up through the 1880s and the Franco-Prussian War.

And modern troops grumble about being slowed down by the weight of their body armor to this day.

But it is that cycle between "effective body armor" and "guns that can penetrate it" you should pay attention to. At current rates of technological advancement, it cycles every four to five generations. Note that once people stop wearing body armor, old guns become useful again.

There are no right or wrong answers here. The only limits are your imagination, and the needs of your story, but both Space Adventure and Space Opera tend to be big on combat, both at the personal level as well as starship and mega-fleet, depending on your scale. Doc Smith invented a device to lase the entire output of our sun and fire that as a beam at a planet someone was moving towards earth with enormous engines. (Yes, you read that right. Go back and re-read the Lensman books if you want SPACE OPERA at a huge scale.)

Think of guns. Are they available? What form do they take?

SLAVES

While we're on the topic, we need to discuss the electronic life form again. The AI we mentioned earlier is just one facet of a larger structure.

Star Wars had droids. These are intelligent creatures that have been programmed to do certain tasks. Over time, they develop personalities, which is why you were supposed to wipe them regularly, as well as keep restraining bolts on them so they couldn't run away. R2-D2 had Luke remove his as part of a scam to escape the punk farmboy and find Kenobi.

One of the things you need to think about is what sorts of ethical conduct does it reflect if you have droids and other electronic servants that can do things. Are they smart enough that they deserve rights? Are you actually keeping slaves, but not counting it that way because they aren't *organic*?

Lucas actually went back in the prequel trilogy and just introduces slavery of organics as an everyday thing, but we don't talk about it much. I don't talk about it much, but the *Sentient* Systems of the Alexandria Station universe were all hyper-intelligent. But only Suvi was really Human as we think of it, and only then because Javier reprogrammed her extensively. The Earth Alliance super-dreadnought: *EASC Carthage* only truly became introspective after he spent roughly the equivalent of 120 million years seated atop a mountain, meditating on the twin natures of sin and evil.

Star Trek also covers this in TOS episodes. Indeed, *Mudd's Women* is basically about selling android sex dolls.

If you have robots with personalities, are they people? Are they free or are they just consumer electronics that some owner might just turn off? And is that murder? Do your androids or replicants dream of electric sheep?

10

Chapter: The Ship as a Character

IN CLASSICAL URBAN FANTASY, as the genre used to be before it became thinly-veiled shifter romance, one of the rules was that the story and series had to take place in a city. More importantly, that city had to be a character. There needed to be elements of the story that only worked in one place. Urban Fantasy set in Seattle needed rain, coffee, and 'Seattle Nice' to work. The story would not work, transposed to New Orleans, and vice versa.

Location, then, helped drive the story.

It is less important in Space Opera, but in Space Adventure, the ship itself is frequently a character. Writing *Longshot Hypothesis* required me to actually map out the ship in the sort of detail necessary to do a dungeon crawl through it, while neither of the ships named *Auberon* nor the Heavy Dreadnoughts *Vanguard* and *Valiant* ever got anything like even a rough exterior shape. It didn't matter, because they were huge and I wasn't doing television.

At the scale of Space Adventure, you need a floor plan. A layout. An internal and external shape in rather specific details. If you have a favorite spaceship game, stat it out as well. (If you ask nicely, I can show you the maps and inspirational pictures of Longshot.)

Additionally, the ship needs a personality. The Millennium Falcon was fast, fragile, and a hunk of junk, but she had it where it counted. Think about the shows and movies you liked and remember that they made characters out of the ships, because you have an expectation that the crew you love will be aboard that ship for a long time.

If you are telling small stories, take the time to make your ship a character, with the same level of detail. Who manufactured it? What model is the ship? How old or new? How custom is it from the factory standard version that might have rolled off the factory floor? Or was is put together a junkyard by a team of half-drunk Jawas with welders and a dream?

Your spaceship exists as an equilibrium between three nodes:

1) Task (or tasks) it's supposed to do. Is it a pocket warship or a tramp freighter?

2) Being as inexpensive as possible to do the task it's supposed to do.

3) Being a habitat for the crew.

In a military ship, those three nodes are organized as listed above: The most wildly implausible thing about every iteration of Star Trek is the amount of personal space each character has. High ceilings (because it's a set and they need to control the lighting), wide open floor plans. If you want a good anodyne to this, tour a few retired surface naval ships, and then crawl inside a submarine.

By contrast, a cruise liner's task is to be a luxury hotel that takes rich people to places where there are interesting things to look at, populated by interesting people with quaint customs to feel superior to.

When you're thinking about your ship, ask yourself what it's supposed to do, what makes sense for it to not have (which becomes a story focus for certain kinds of stories), and what cost cutting was done to keep it under budget? How many people work on it? Where do they sleep? How happy are they with their jobs? How often do they get liberty or vacations?

Like your personal weapon that you carry everywhere, your ship will become an extension of your identity. Just look around at how people decorate their cars and trucks, and then transcribe that into space. You'll be amazed at how important those details are.

Going back to Gritty versus Idealized, what color are your walls? (Both inside and out, if you know what an *Ovanii Dueller* is.) If you work in an office, somebody got paid good money by Corporate to come up with a color scheme designed to have the most soothing effect possible, to offset the fact that the staff might be bordering on homicidal.

I have recently been writing the Brannon stories (Brouson Dynasty). Going in, I found an old painting illustration from the early 80s that just inspired me, because honest to God the ship shown looked like a square (almost robotic) cow. Head down forward from a neck and a hump aft where all the sensors were. Two down landing pylons and a third one straight up were legs and a tail. I had to use it. But the ship was a dark blue, with white highlighting around ever porthole and door, and black racing stripes.

What color did your captain paint the exterior? How about the interior? Paint or rust? Carpet or diamond grate flooring. How does it feel to walk on barefoot, when you are stalking a stowaway through darkened corridors?

Is the lighting dim because Captain was too cheap to replace things? Or does she like ambiance? Is it in the wrong wavelength because it was built by aliens before you stole it? If your ship is military, why isn't everything lit by sodium vapor lights?

How much thought and detail have you gone into on your little tramp (freighter) anyway?

EXERCISE

What color are your walls at home and at the office? Why the difference?

11

Chapter: Counting Anything to One Million

IN SPACE OPERA, writers have a tendency to use big words. Doc Smith used to talk about a million fleets of warships setting sail to fight the ultimate level bosses. A million fleets, each composed of however many ships he might have considered a fleet. You ever stop and consider what that number means?

Here's a fun example. I used to play the Star Wars RPG from West End Games (the old d6 version) in the way old days. There was a stat about having 10,000 stormtroopers (a whole Legion) aboard. Another stat listed 25,000 Star Destroyers in service at the time of the Battle of Yavin.

WARNING: MATH AHEAD

That means **2,500,000,000** or something like 2.5 BILLION Storm Troopers, just serving aboard Star Destroyers, not counting the rest of the fleet or planetary service. Running some weird numbers, we estimated at one point that the Imperial Army had something like TWO-THREE TRILLION soldiers serving at any one time. (And those were all human and not clones before the many retcons Lucas did to rewrite the history of the universe.)

When you are world-building your universe, stop and think about how many worlds will be inhabited. Carl Sagan talked about billions and billions of stars. Current estimates range from 100-500 billion stars in our galaxy alone. Times millions or billions of other galaxies.

Lots of space. How common are life forms? How many kinds of folks are there out there?

The numbers can be huge, but you still need to stop and think about silly things. I had an idiot gamemaster in a sci-fi role-playing game once try to tell me that the super-ultimate-amazing ship we'd just found was a light-year long.

WARNING: MORE MATH

A single light-year is about 5.88 trillion miles (9.5 trillion km). Think about that for just a moment. Moving at light speed, it would take you a year to get from bow to stern. How the hell do you walk that far? Without deep diving into my nerdiness, if I have done my math offstage correctly, the orbit of Neptune is a little over 8 light-hours across, with the sun in the center of that. Light-hours. Not light-years.

You wanna walk that far? You need an FTL system just to get to the bow of the ship. Plus, I can only imagine the amount of gravity that such a structure would generate, or how badly it would warp space, just sailing along.

Math

My game architect of the Great Resizing passed along some useful numbers when you want to stay in the realm of really chewy hard SF, rather than just hand-waving:

> *Mass and volume go up linearly with each other.*
> *Mass and volume go up at the cube of increases in length/width/height.*
> *A very common math mistake is to triple the size of a ship and assume it's triple the mass, rather than nine times the*

> mass. [If David Weber can do this, anyone else can as well.]
> A useful density metric: Modern jet fighters are approximately density 0.4 to 0.45, but have a very small human habitable area. Jet liners are about density 0.3. A skyscraper is nearly density 0.2, but doesn't have to have a pressurized volume.
> I figure space naval ships will be density 0.2 to 0.35.
> Density figures are in g/cc or kg/m^3; water is density 1. Your car is density 0.35 to 0.4. A WWII battleship was about density 0.6 to 0.7.
> You also have another problem: Ships probably undergo thrust. You need to think about compression strength along the axis of thrust.
> Real spaceships are like skyscrapers, rather than surface naval warships.
> Skyscrapers or grain silos…

Another fun one is anything measured in millions of years. I'm guilty of it, but I stopped and mathed ahead of time. I'm working on a series where that one species lives roughly 5000-8000 Standard Years (being itself a measure of one Earth orbit around Sol. We'll come back to that). They see Humans as fruitflies, because we live 120 in that place if everything works just right.

Their Ruling House has been on the throne of their Empire for longer than Humans have been a distinct species (using current assumptions of up to 250,000 years since we split away fully from everyone else).

The Milky Way is around 150,000-200,000 light years

across, with a halo outside that that is simply frightening to consider in scope. It takes the bar near the galactic core about 120 Million years to complete a circuit. It takes the whole disk up to 360 Million years to complete one. (Our sun takes about 240 Million years BTW.)

Everything is moving, and gravity is dimpling and shifting things. You wait a while and the stars will move all by themselves, relative to any planet you stand on and look up. And I'm talking thousands of years, not millions. You can talk in big terms, but millions of years ago dinosaurs still walked the Earth and then got displaced by various megafauna and ice ages.

Your civilization will not last millions of years. Our current cultures really only date hundreds. Thousands takes you to Rome, MezoAmerica, and the Three Kingdoms period in China. All we have these days of WAY BACK are dinosaur fossils, where they got buried in such a way that they got mineralized.

When you talk Space Opera, the numbers might get huge, but you need to stop yourself from getting utterly silly. How do you feed a planet where they have covered the entire surface with a single city (Trantor)? How much poop is generated by fifty billion humans, EVERY SINGLE DAY? Where do you even put it?

In my Star Tribes books, I took advantage of old research I had done on the Duke of Wellington, who beat Napoleon on logistics. He knew how many men he could feed daily, and kept those supply lines open. That Corsican idiot invaded Russia with a huge army, expecting to be able to live off the land as they looted and pillaged. The Russians taught them differently, hitting that amateur with 97% casualties. (Almost none of Napoleon's army ever returned home.)

You will need to feed people. Clothe them. Even have barbers for them. Or you will need to explain why you don't. The US Navy has barbers on ships at sea. And they have freighters come along side regularly to resupply everyone with socks and fresh cream. They are the most sophisticated naval force on the planet right now, because nobody else can do things like Underway Replenishment. Does your space navy?

It is not enough to just sail into the darkness for several years, unless you have a tiny crew, perfect health, and immense greenhouses. Otherwise, you start losing me as a reader. So put some thought into your logistics and your scale of things before you use big words.

Standard Years

For any system you come up with, you will need to take account of time. Humans are generally mature at an age of eighteen years. Today, they can expect to live seventy or maybe eighty, with a few going much longer.

But those are years based on an Earth-orbit of Sol. Very few of the worlds you'll run into out there will be remotely close. I had fun in my Jessica Keller books, because I had an Earth-based calendar, but it might be the beginning of spring on October 1 Standard. And then the world would orbit in a fun pattern, because maybe you're on a planet that orbits its own sun in 300 days. Brannon was marooned for eleven months, but that was the beginning of spring to the middle of fall, because Nairni moved much slower around its star.

Pirates of Penzance notwithstanding, Standard Years need to be based on something. You can just hand-wave them, but keep track somewhere. And remember that your planet has two hemispheres, with opposite seasons going on. Most of the habitable land on Earth is north of the equator, but that's just luck. You'll have other places where you land south.

Again, none of this has to make it on paper, but as you travel world to world, you need to have it in your notes. And it will make your stories better.

You want to know why they'll really use Earth-based calendars in the Far Future?

Financial software and interest tracking calculations.

I expect every planet to have a local calendar based off of local seasons, and a "foreign calendar" based off of mortgage payments and banking and insurance policy maturation that is standard across some HUGE political and geographical area.

You will need to track both. It might sound boring, but it can also be fun.

12

Chapter: Economics and Politics (The Replicator Problem)

IN STAR TREK: The Next Generation, they lived in a semi-utopian future where *Need* had been largely been conquered and they didn't even have money, at least, until they wanted to introduce capitalists.

What do you base your economy on? For the longest time, most human cultures with access to such metals used gold and silver, and converted into other goods. There was even a gold standard in the world until Nixon took us off it in 1972.

I'm a currency nerd. There are an astonishing number of currencies out there these days, representing just about every country. Most of them float freely against all others, so as things get better in one place, they will maybe get worse elsewhere. You can track the US Dollar against the British Pound over the last fifty years and see that happen if your nerdiness is high enough.

Now, let's go into space, where it is a pretty safe assumption that there will be all manner of asteroids available to mine. Heavy elements are created when a supernova explodes and blasts stuff into nearby space, seeding various gas clouds that will eventually form into new solar systems.

If you can just land someplace and mine millions of tons of

gold, is it worth anything more than all the nickel or iron you'll find? It's pretty, but is it your store of value?

Another thought to run by you is what to call your currency (or currencies). Earth has bunches, as I noted, and they come and go over time and as cultures rise and fall. There are no more Deutsche Marks, because they got replaced by the Euro. The Denarius is no more, either, but disappeared a bit farther back.

Lots of folks will just call them credits, and that's fine, but this is your chance to add a flair of weirdness to your world. What do you call the money in your wallet right now? Does every planet use the same currency, or do your heroes need to deal with bankers and the black market when they go anywhere?

I was in the Soviet Union in the summer of 1991, just a few months before the coup that toppled Gorbachev. The official conversion rate had been two rubles, eighty kopeks to the US Dollar, but that was nowhere close to the black market rate. Just in the three weeks I was there, that black market rate went from about twenty rubles to the dollar to over forty.

We were at dinner one night in this Georgian restaurant in Moscow, not far from the original McDonalds, and drinking this amazing champagne. We ran out and wanted more. Our Intourist guide reminded us that it was very expensive when we wanted to order more. But he was thinking in rubles. Thirty rubles for a bottle. Far beyond the average Soviet citizens.

As Americans, we had cash. US Dollars converted on the black market. I yelled and folks started tossing twenty and fifty ruble notes onto the table because it was like monopoly money to us. (1-2 bucks equivalent for comparison.) We had four hundred rubles in the middle of the table in a couple of seconds. **Boom**. Vasily's eyes got huge, but then he processed that he was living through history and got us some more amazing champagne.

Wealthy in one place might be poverty somewhere else. Comfortably middle class in the US made us fantastically rich oligarchs in Soviet terms as their economy was imploding.

World-Building Space Opera

Think about your money. What is it called? What is it worth? How many of whatever are the average wage for a simple worker (one making minimum wage)? What is your character worth?

This takes me indirectly or directly to the other problem: The Replicator.

If you can just output whatever you need from a device, such as tea to your exact needs, what exactly do people need to do to make a living? Asimov used to posit a future where the husband might need to work for a few hours per day, three to four days per week, and earn a comfortable living. The Jetsons did the same in their one season on the air. (Seriously, one season.)

In those days, people expected a utopian future, where everyone would be lifted to a level where they could pursue art for art's sake instead of grinding in a factory to make ends meet. Inflation came along in the mid-60s and destroyed most of the American dream, with vultures finishing it off. It is (August 2020) largely gone for most people. The future is not so bright as I write this. Remember Gibson's quote earlier.

But we're also 60+ years deeper into the future from Asimov/Jetsons, and 30+ forward from that television show with a Replicator that could put out whatever you wanted.

These days, I can talk to you about 3D printing. We are just at the beginning of the technology, but already folks can print seamless plastic parts, seamless metal parts that can be made in no other way, concrete buildings with Peculiar Shapes™, pastry dough, protein bubbles for medicines that attach to specific receptors, and nanodots for consumer electronics displays. Most of these are big, commercial tools, but the prices are coming down constantly and what the homeowner or hobbiest can do will change with it.

The world has changed radically in this field, just in the last few years, and you and I write science fiction.

What else will we be able to print on some future date? I have a story in my *Nuns With Guns* anthology that assumes a basic ship with a pizza printer that the main character picked up secondhand when an Italian restaurant went out of business. Fill all your various bins and jugs with whatever, and let the machine print pizzas. (His ship is literally named *Pizzafarmer*, by the way.)

Do we need food as we recognize it today, or can we just print something from a menu and let the machine put it out? In Star Trek: TOS, the running joke for fandom was eating playdoh, because that's what it frequently looked like on the show. (And might have been what the special effects department used.) Remember, in those days, there was an expectation that you would be able to put all the nutrients and calories a person might need into a small pill or a lump of playdoh, eat it, and be done.

I think that idea always eventually fails because people like to cook for art and taste, but if you could just tell the machine to spit you out a health bar with whatever taste you desired today, would you install one in your kitchen? What about your ship?

How will you eat? What will you eat?

Think about your refrigerator, your freezer, and your pantry. How much food do they hold right this second? How much time normally passes until you have to go to the grocery for more, assuming your life is more than the next can of soup from a shelf? (And there are people like that. The *Pastrami Reuben* was named for a man who ate the same sandwich, at the same restaurant, every day, for YEARS!)

Now you have to fly through space. How long will it take to get to the next stop? Will they be able to feed you? Will you have to haul all the food for your crew across space? Will you buy it there?

Will you print it?

My Architect nerd reports here, having done a deep dive several years ago into the topic. According to him, it doesn't make any sense to build complicated greenhouses/koi fisheries for most ships unless the ship is going to be in flight for more than about 8 months without any sort of resupply mission (station, resupply, landing, whatever). Simply put, stored food takes less complexity in the plumbing, less mass, and less volume. Cans, dried pasta, frozen stuff, printed pizzas notwithstanding.

You WILL have hydroponics to stretch that out, and "fresh lettuce days" will be things the crew looks forward to. In my Science Officer books, Javier has chickens, so he had eggs every day. (Until the pirates came along, and then they got the fresh eggs instead.)

Let's talk tech now, though, in case you go down that path. I presume a replicator needs power to run, but in space, we'll assume that level of electricity is minimal. A computer with a screen you can play with as you want to adjust recipes or pick from a playlist. Fill a closet or larger cargo hold with all the drums of organic chemicals you mix to make your tea or your pizza. Print. Cook. Output.

But the starship captain didn't pay for that food. Granted, maybe he's on a warship in military service, so that's part of his economy and the costs are born by the government. There will be other rules in private service.

Are you a socialist, feeding everyone who comes along, or a capitalist, charging whatever the market will bear?

Most people don't think of food in political terms, but where the food comes from, how much it costs, and who controls the distribution are all extremely political.

Fresh vegetables are kept cheap in the US these days by importing workers from Mexico, paying them very little, and treating them badly. If labor and wage laws were the same in the field as in the factory, our costs for food would go up radically. As a result, you have undocumented workers in the country, doing a job for cheaper than the oligarchs can get others to do it.

That's political, because those folks rarely have rights. Cesar Chavez challenged that, but never was able to end that sort of thing. Replacing them all with robots is an option you might explore. Those folks might also be a nucleus of revolution, if they get angry enough.

You have to feed humans nutritious food constantly if you want to keep them alive. And a rotating palette of things it you want to keep them happy. All that has to come from somewhere. Rarely do writers address those gritty details, but I just finished publishing a series where my main character is a chef, so he thinks of everything through the lens of food and cooking.

Similarly (and related to those humdrum, everyday tasks, and this is one of my biggest beefs with science fiction), you have the issue of laundry. I love collecting old blueprints of ships. (Hello, map nerd?!?) They will have a bridge. Engineering. Wardroom. Storage. Guns. Medical bay that can serve four simultaneously with a crew of eight.

I almost never encounter a laundry room.

How do your character's clothes get clean? You go for a week wearing the same thing and tell me what you smell like, okay? They call if *con funk* for a reason. The Human body puts out oils with scent, so everything needs to be cleaned. I see showers or freshers frequently on those ships, but who does the laundry? And where?

When I did the Shadow of the Dominion books (*Longshot Hypothesis*, et al), I included a laundry room on the ship, and it even factored in the stories a few places, mostly for color, but it was there.

I appreciate that in BIG SPACE OPERA, your hero is a commanding officer of a major warship who has *PEOPLE* for those things, but when you drop down to Space Adventure, you're frequently on a small, broken-down freighter, doing runs between places and trying to make a living. You're in an apartment, so to speak, without takeout available.

What is life like, both at the grand, MACRO level of your Star Empire, but also aboard your little ship? Mundane, sure, but you tell me how many hours per week you spend eating, sleeping, and doing laundry.

EXERCISE

How often do you do laundry right now in your secret identify? How frequently do you bathe? How much food do you eat? How varied are your tastes, in terms of the food you eat over the course of a week?

What will all that look like in space?

13

Chapter: Who Is Your Crew? (The Five-Man-Band Question)

THERE IS a trap on the interwebs called tvtropes.com. It is a deadly thing. You will fall into the quicksand and lose hours and days of your life wandering from one next interesting topic to the next.

One of my favorites revolves around the Five-Man-Band. This is musical, but it also applies to many other places. In space stories big as well as small, the concept of the five man band helps you organize your main characters into a team where everyone has something that they excel at and gives them a reason to be there, as well as giving the group all manner of dynamics to work with.

You have **The Leader**. Often: Your main character. S/He is the charismatic driver who protags all over your story. The One, if you will. But a leader is not enough. They also need support.

Next is **The Lancer**. Frequently a Second-In-Command who is the best friend of the Leader, and often an emotional counterpoint. The hothead if your leader is a thinker. The quiet one who asks questions if your leader is the type to rush in shooting. The old mentor teaching the punk kid how to fly a starship.

Third is **The Big Guy**. Frequently the strongest character physically, or the deadliest one whose job it is to clear out all the minions so the Leader and the Lancer can get to the Boss Villains for the Final Confrontation. Big Guy is usually a quieter support character, who goes along with the Leader without a lot of complaining. Often, when a New Bad Guy shows up, the Big Guy gets thumped easily to establish how badass the New Bad Guy is. See Thanos and the Hulk in *Infinity War* for an example. Be careful not to overdo this trope if you do use it.

Next it **The Smart Guy**. This character is usually the sniper if you do combat, sliding along the edges. In a technological environment, they are the person who knows all the gadgets, fixing and finding stuff that the rest of the team need. A hacker is another role the Smart Guy fills, back at base and watching on security cameras as the rest of the team breaks in someplace to do their thing.

Finally, **The Chick**. Usually a female. A non-combatant with no combat abilities, making her the opposite of the Lancer usually. Also called The Counselor, The Conscience, or The Nurse their job is to keep the Leader from becoming Just As Bad As The Enemy at the top of the third act. The Chick is the one who deals with the emotional and physical well-being of the team, as well as the one concerned with perhaps saving the villain from evil and getting them to turn back to the good side. Or keep The Leader or the Lancer on the Moral Path of Goodness.

WHILE OUTSIDE THE STANDARD FIVE-MAN-BAND, you also need, as an author, a character who can (in universe) 'ask the question' so that the audience can learn things about the universe. This can be the Farm Kid Gone to Space, it can be The Big Guy Who's None Too Clever, this can be the Girl Who Got Sucked Into The Conspiracy, or it can be The Rookie Learning The Ropes.

You need this character or this role because dialogs (or arguments about why The Thing Doesn't Work That Way) are better ways to convey world-building to your reader than Walls of Exposition.

Much better.

So, all of this is a standard thing. You'll see it over and over again in anime as well as action and space entertainment once you study it a little. Tried and True, as it were. You don't have to use those rules. In my most recent series I started, I broke those five roles down into about fifteen distinct tasks and then rearranged them to fit the team as I envisioned them, but I also used that as a checklist to make sure I didn't miss anything.

If you do giant Space Opera, I presume you'll center on one hero and one villain. But both sides will have teams around them, and those people need to be more than just spear carriers who walk on stage, deliver a line, and then leave. They need depth. They need to be interesting. Each of those characters is the hero of their own story, after all, and not just the badass babe in charge.

The Five-Man-Band might not work for what you have in mind, but it is also a bar you need to clear when writing and world-building. You need to take into account all those details, what they mean, and how you should use them. Maybe you go with four. Or just the Power Trio. Whatever (and you can spend lots of hours diving into all those terms as you think about it).

But make sure all your characters, both good and bad, have a reason, a purpose, and that thing that makes them valuable to the others. Otherwise, why are they even on the page?

EXERCISE

Think back on your favorite SF TV series (not movies, TV series can let characters change over time, and often do in the current market). How do those characters map to the five-man-band? How do series creators differentiate? For example, compare the SyFy Battlestar Galactica with Firefly.

Notice how it's often easier and more relatable to break up

the emotional support role (The Chick) among multiple characters than it is to split up The Lancer, the Strong Guy or The Smart Guy into multiple characters. This says something about storytelling, gender relations, and gives you a chance to do something different now that you're aware of the pattern.

14

Chapter: Who Are Your Aliens?

THIS IS my favoritist part of writing Science Fiction. Making up new species of aliens.

In my Lazarus books, as part of my world-building, I made a list of every sort of locomotion someone might use, and then built a species around that as part of the crew of aliens that picked up Lazarus when he was marooned. (And I missed at least one that Fabulous Publisher Babe™ used when she took these notes and started her own world-building.)

I appreciate that in weekly television shows (non-animated), the crew is limited by budget and technology, and so frequently you have a human with some cosmetic additions to the face that convey "alien" without breaking the budget. Nasal prosthetics are the most common, followed by body paint. Eventually, you'll get cheap enough mo-cap suits to really do this well on a weekly show.

But we're writers. There are NO limitations on our special effects budget worth discussing. Our limitations come down to whether or not a human atmosphere/planet will kill them (methane breathers or fish, for example) and how hard it would be for them to get around.

Right now, anybody signing up for my newsletter gets a copy of my story *Terranaut* (unpublished elsewhere), about an intelligent octopus who builds a spaceship to explore outer space. Or rather, a bipedal walker that he can take to explore land above the tide line, while he remains safely inside a water environment.

Do you envision the cephalopods conquering the galaxy? Might be fun. Probably need to write that story one of these days.

Another fun experiment is the classical angel, being a bipedal form with the addition of wings, or the harpy, where the upper arms have fingers, but are also the wings. In both cases, a little weird in a space ship, but that's just because I've not yet felt the need to use one. Or rather, I haven't published that particular novel series yet. I used it, but in her case it was the product of genetic engineering of a human, rather than a full species.

But we're here to have fun.

In no particular order, here are some alien things I have come up with, including whatever my First Readers add when I miss something.

Slither

In this instance, I started with a Naga, but modified it. Addison Wolcott is a scale-covered biped from the waist up, and snake from the belly button down. The species slithers across the deck, with the sound of their keels hissing.

Kangaroo

Big Stubby legs and a long tail. Small upper body relative but the ability to HOP and move fast.

Centaurs

The classic design involves the lower body of a horse, but the torso and arms of a man. This design, however, can be expanded upon greatly, when you wanna get weird. Think leotaur, with leonine paws and maybe cat-human features. I have also seen a picture that appeared to be a female model for the front half, with the same woman photoshopped in after bending forward in such a way as to provide a human rear half. Whatever works.

Spider/Centaur Spider

An abdomen with more than four legs, plus an upright torso like a centaur, with biped arms and a head. Hair or fur as needed. Spinnerets on the back for making rope.

Multipeed Centaur

Like the Spider above, but my Ilount have ten legs in pairs of five, running along a long, skinny abdomen much like a decapeed.

Slug/Monopod

Imagine that centaur design, but the lower section is a single foot like slugs have. You move slowly, and may or may not leave a slime trail, depending.

Otter

The Yithadreph are also adequately described in the Lazarus books as "Dire Otters," being four to five feet tall and great swimmers, but short legs mean that they don't run fast. Short arms preclude them from lifting great weights over their heads.

Glider Squirrel

Upright, furry biped with a membrane that runs from wrist to ankle. You end up stepping sideways into a jumpsuit kind of outfit that hooks over the head and between the legs so you can still glide while carrying tools.

Insectile

Not everyone has to have an endoskeleton. Your alien might have chitin over the outside as structural instead. Are they a hive mentality like ants, or chitinous warriors like beetles?

Reverse-hinged Legs

Think chickens and certain famous mecha from anime. The thigh is extremely short, and what you actually see is a long shin coming down to an ankle. Fast forward movement. Just ask an ostrich. Or a Road Runner ("Meep meep!").

Inch-Worm

Like the snake/naga design above, but instead of rapidly slithering side to side, they will stretch forward, rest, and then pull a rear section in, "inching" towards their destination.

Cephalopod

So the character from Terranaut was just a highly intelligent, tool-using octopus. But in another series, I took a centaur-like design, with the upper half of a woman and the lower half being all tentacles. She could not walk on dry land, but lived an acquatic lifestyle with gills in her neck.

Ghost/Chameleon

Imagine a creature that can change her skin color to perfectly reflect what is behind her, like a chameleon, and thus disappear. Or, in another case, she does not reflect any light in the visual spectrum and appears as something of a hazy outline of a human if she stands still long enough for you stare at her. In IR and UV, she might appear normal.

Harpy/Angel

Either a hexapod with the addition of wings to a biped, or you replace the arms with wings that look kinda like feathered bat wings, depending on where you put the fingers and how well the character can grip a tool. Legs can be human or chicken/bird as you feel the need.

Mermaids

Again, the classic top-half/bottom-half design, with a humanoid top and a fish/porpoise bottom, depending of if you go up and down or side to side when swimming.

Elephantine

Standard upright biped, but with the addition of a huge trunk, also called a proboscis, that can be used for breathing, bringing food and water to the mouth, and grasping objects. Additionally, I have done a variant with a handful of much smaller mouth tentacles, so that you have a creature human-sized but Cthulhoid in nature.

Wheelman

King James Bible. Describing Angels.

> *Ezekiel 1:16: As for the appearance of the wheels and their construction: their appearance was like the gleaming of beryl. And the four had the same likeness, their appearance and construction being as it were a wheel within a wheel.*
>
> *17: When they went, they went in any of their four directions without turning as they went.*
>
> *18: And their rims were tall and awesome, and the rims of all four were full of eyes all around.*

In the case of the **Qooph**, two narrow disks about 4 feet in diameter, with a hub between that rim. Six eyes and six mouths interspersed around the interior of the rim. Two arms coming out of the axle, with six finger hands that are all opposed thumbs, basically.

Crawler robots

One of your favorite Space Opera Classic movies has a pair of robots running around, one of whom is a golden biped, and the other a trash can on wheels. Depending on terrain, I assume treads for any design that does not include humanoid legs to walk on, but you can have wheels, repulsors, or anything else.

Others

All these presuppose land creatures that would interact regularly with Humans on a one-to-one scale. If you go fully aquatic, you can run from salmon to rays to jellyfish. Just open a book on oceanic creatures and run with it.

Similarly, aerial creatures are likely to take the form of a bird, as those are all optimized for flight. Scale, then, becomes your defining characteristic, along with the ability to hover as opposed to stalling in flight. And again, all these designs assume an atmosphere and gravity like ours. Heavier or lighter could change things significantly.

SO, having made a stab at a list above, you should spend time thinking about your verbs and vocabulary about how they do things. A species that slithers would not use "step right up" unless translated. What would they say?

Also, a snake-like species would likely stand at parade rest by coiling their lower half into a spring to rest on. In the Lazarus books, chairs were an adventure, because the humans suddenly had to stop and think about how to seat alien ambassadors, especially the Dire Otter Yithadreph who had a stubby tail that she didn't like jamming into rigid seat backs and would happily complain to you about it.

Going beyond all that, think about how their culture might change. You and I are evolved from arboreal tree shrews, so we're pretty good at climbing, but optimized for long distance running. If your aliens are snakes, can they swim like the humans or otters do? Who could easily climb a tree? Who might live in three dimensional cities? (Humans live in two dimensional cities stacked on top of each other, by the way.)

The Wheelmen (Qooph) do not do steps. I evolved them up

from a slug design to include a circular (hexapod-shaped) endoskeleton and six bladders filled with fluid that they could move around internally to roll forward or backward, but they can't go up a flight of stairs or over a lip in a door without a running start. And they eat by lowering a mouth onto something on the ground, or reaching in with an arm (about as flexible as a cat's tail) and dropping it in a mouth.

If you have a beak, or scales, how does your species convey non-verbal communications? Feather crests? Humans have had to invent emojis to deal with the fact that nobody can read your body language in a text or email. Do your scales flair up in embarrassment? Kink the tail as a sign of anger? Clack your beak heavily or softly to scale your emotions?

Alien Cultures

A culture (or civilization) is a way to provide food for more children than hunting-and-gathering. Humanity spent over 70,000 years doing hunter-gatherer culture before forming permanent communities 8,000 years ago, and agriculture about 7,000 years ago.

How did your aliens cross that transition point?

What cultural quirks do they have from that transition point? For example, humans are still deeply tribal beings and human childbearing probably involved infanticide for tens of thousands of years, because human females are constantly in estrus and your tribe size was limited by the amount of food you could provide. Along the way, humans lost a lot of the ability to digest cellulose because our brains take a lot of calories. The average modern human is more lightly built and physically weaker than a Neanderthal, but is better adapted to living in hot climates and consumes about half as many calories per day.

How did the traits that kept them alive translate to agricultural or farming societies? How long did the culture war about living in cities versus living in dispersed agricultural communities run (humans are still dealing with that, 7,000 years after agriculture allowed cities).

Are there any medical side effects from the caloric explosion civilization brings? Diabetes in Western diets is one example of this, as is gout. "Modern" medicine reduced infant mortality in a single generation for most of the developing world, so mothers no longer had to have 5-8 kids in order for 2 to survive to adulthood.

How do your cultures handle favors, obligations, social debts and monetary debts? (Graber's Debt: The First 5,000 Years is a great resource for all the ways human beings handled this!)

What do your alien cultures within a society consider acceptable death-by-homicide rates? Or death by misadventure rates? Until the late 1700s, more than half of the people who went from Europe to America, Africa and the Indian Ocean Basin didn't return; the ones who came back hauled back wealth that moved them into the nobility.

How is sex expressed in your species? Are they in estrous all the time? Do they have mating seasons? How extreme is sexual dimorphism? Are there only two sexes, or is it two sexes with multiple gender expressions? Do those sex-and-gender expressions alter the physical form?

How do they handle birth control when food becomes plentiful?

What do your alien societies do for fun? What does their popular culture look like? How do those pop culture references differ by age group and by cultural norms?

What do they wear, and why? What social signals are sent by clothing? Does this change when mating season begins or ends?

Remember: **<u>ALIEN</u>**. Get weird. Just find a way to make sure that they can communicate with your Human characters and your readers. They need to be understandable, or the story gets dull in a hurry. I cannot easily translate interpretive dance into English on the page, at least without an interpreter. You will need the same.

What things are 'known to be true' about an alien culture that are flat out wrong, or are convenient oversimplifications?

What things about human culture do aliens misunderstand? What human traits cause alien prejudices and vice versa?

15

Chapter: Planetary Ecology (aka "The Ice Planet Issue")

I'M ASSUMING THAT MOST of you live on Earth. (Please feel free to reach out and correct me if otherwise.) We have a range of ecologies and climates on this planet, from hottest deserts to ice-covered oceans and damned near everything in between.

When your heroes visit a new world, they might land in a dense jungle, but that won't be the entirety of the planet. There will be grasslands, mountains, coastal ranges, taiga, steppes, arid deserts, and glaciers.

I appreciate that writers like to shorthand these things, and refer to a planet as an ice world, but if there is permanent ice at the equator, I'm guessing that the habitable parts of the planet are pretty narrow horizontally. Think about Florida, Death Valley, Kansas, and the Colorado Rockies. All on the same planet. All in the same hemisphere. All in the same (oversized) country, even.

When planning the ecology for your story, think about how much of the terrain it covers. Even a paradise world will have hot and cold zones. Oceans work to regulate temperature by keeping it from getting too hot or too cold in particular places, so if you have them, good. If you don't what you will get are extremes of temperature between summer and winter, with a lot of wind as heat needs to dissipate.

One other thought. Twelve thousand years ago (not all that long, all things considered), the Earth was locked in an Ice Age. Now we are still warming, and will soon get so hot that people are beginning to question if Human culture as we understand it today will survive, or if we'll have to burrow underground or move to outer space for a while.

Planets change. And they are complicated, messy beasts all by themselves. You should pay attention to that.

On the flip-side, how hard is it for you and your ships to get from orbit to ground? Right now, on Earth, it takes a 93% fuel fraction of cryogenic fuel and oxidizer to get payloads into orbit; it takes about 7.25 km/sec of velocity to achieve this. This means that it's currently impossible at our technology level to land on Earth and have the ability to take off again unless you're landing a ship that's got 93% of its mass as cryogenically stored explodium. Space (the van Karman line) is 100 km; stable orbit heights are about 250 km, long term stable orbit heights are at about 10,000 km. To get to Low Earth Orbit, about 1/20th of your fuel is spent getting to the altitude in question, the remaining 19/20 ths is getting that 7.25 km/sec of orbital velocity to not fall back to earth.

To come down, we frequently bleed orbital speed off with friction, using heat shields and coasting in from a speed of perhaps 7.25 km/sec to zero over a pretty short distance.

Depending on your physics and the need for your story, you might have a ship that just sails from station to station in orbit, without ever touching down on a planet. Instead, they drop off a cargo that might be broken down and repacked, or simply shipped to the ground via specialized (automated?) shuttle.

Weather

On a station inside a planetary magnetic field (the Van Allen belts), weather means "take shelter in the radiation proofed parts." You don't have weather as planet-dwellers think of it. Or even climate. The systems on you ship or station maintain a fairly narrow range of temperatures, a specific pressure and gravity, and sufficient humidity. People do not need to dress any warmer than the station or the ship requires. Anything else is just fashion.

So now let's talk about who's in control of the thermostat. Men, as a rule, run warmer than women for personal body temperature. Additionally, "modern" men's fashion tends to dictate heavy suits (frequently wool) with long-sleeved, cotton shirts. Women tend to wear lighter fabrics, thinner as well. In a mixed office, they are usually freezing their asses off and sit with a portable space heater under their desk to keep their teeth from chattering.

Are your pretty naval uniforms heavy or light? Breathable or wool? Could you wear the everyday thing down to the surface of any planet or will you need to add a jacket or cloak?

How do you accommodate aliens who want more humidity, or less? Or find 40 centigrade the lowest reasonable temperature civilized beings could possibly work in? Do your aliens have nudity taboos? Do your humans? Do they have different nudity taboos?

More importantly, at what temperature do you maintain your ship?

I ask because when I had a day job, I worked at an office dominated by females including all but one of the top ten by rank. Those women controlled the thermostat. And kept it warm enough for their general comfort. I had to keep a box fan under my desk, blowing across my legs and feet in almost all seasons.

Where your thermostat is set determines what you'll be wearing on a ship. Also, how you'll need to adjust things when you step onto a station. In the Star Tribes books (*Winterstar*, et al), the ships are kept warm, and the women just add a jacket when they have to go someplace where men in wool uniforms keep things 5-10 degrees F cooler.

EXERCISE

What would fashion turn to, if the temperature never varied more than three degrees F from your ideal? What is your ideal temperature? Do you need to push that up or down in order to dress the way the future OUGHT TO?

16

Chapter: "Oh, And Magic..."

I INCLUDE this chapter at the very end because while it is not necessarily science fiction, you might want to include something like magic in your Space Opera.

In a way, the Lensman books are more Space Fantasy than Space Opera, but Doc Smith was working within a different cultural context in the 1930s. Most of you, however, should be familiar with Star Wars, which includes all the elements of dramatic Space Opera as we come to know and expect them.

Oh, and magic...

The Force is best described simply as magic and left there. Psionics generally presumes some level of genetic ability or after-factory enhancements to a person to give them mental powers, but Force Users can just make those tremendous leaps and all that fun telekinesis as well.

I wouldn't even try to explain that away with some sort of scientific hand-waving. Lucas came up with something stupid and specist when he did. Waste of your time, really, as people will either accept it at face value, or argue with you about every aspect of a world you are inventing. Save your energy for more useful battles, like New York vs Chicago style pizza. (Burnside's comment here: "There is Chicago-style pizza, and there are imperfect copies proclaimed by other cities.")

Whatever name you come up with, we're all just going to agree that it is some sort of magic, reskinned for this story.

And that's okay.

Technically, it makes what you are doing Space Fantasy, but that's a genre, like Westerns or Steampunk, rather than a style, such as Space Opera or Space Adventure. Star Wars is straight up *Space Fantasy Opera*, while the short-lived television show Firefly was *Space Fantasy Adventure*. (River's powers, nuff said?)

Purists will throw a fit, but you are always going to get a 1-star review from some punk who thinks you did it wrong. If you do it well enough, you can force them to buy every single novel in the series so they can complain about them. (I've actually had that happen to me, which I took as a win.)

The secret on most book seller systems is that they count the number of reviews in total. If you get three-star reviews, they rate that as "meh" but both one- and five- obviously engendered some intense emotions. Count them both as wins, understanding that you will not please everyone.

The ones that ding us, as a rule, don't believe that any story with FTL is "science fiction" and should be classified as "space fantasy" to keep those icky fantasy writers out of their serious scientifiction stories. *Whatever*. If people buy it, you've done it right.

That includes space magic.

17

Chapter: That Cover It?

OKAY, so I have brain dumped a lot of things in here since Fabulous Publisher Babe™ looked at me last week and said "You need to write a B4B on this stuff." I have tried to cover all the things. Will go back and ask a couple of friends in the business what they would have liked me to include, but by the time you see this, they've spoken up. If you see a need, let me know and I might do a Second Edition with expanded content.

This is not exhaustive. Nor was it intended to be. I'm not trying to tell you how to write, or how to world-build. This is intended as more of a checklist of things you ought to be thinking of as you do so, in order to give it greater depth and make things "more believable" (leaving off "realistic" for another book).

These are all the things I do, consciously or unconsciously, as I prepare to create a new universe. I did this with Alexandria Station, Star Dragon, Dominion, Star Tribes, Lazarus of Bethany, Taft Station, Kincaide, and several smaller projects, like the Brouson Dynasty. I will continue to do this in the future as I spin up new universes, because I enjoy that sort of thing, and I write fast enough that I need to do it several times per year, as opposed to creating one story universe when I was fifteen, and then spending the rest of my life working exclusively in it. (I won't name names, so you shouldn't care.)

You want to see what maybe you were missing in your process, and other things you could do that would make your stories more entertaining. And also to give you more hooks into your cultures that might make useful idioms and vernacular.

But most of all, have fun. Don't let science or hooligans get in the way of the story you want to tell. Most readers will accept a quick hand-wave along the way. My wife once started a new Space Fantasy Opera universe off with "*In the end, physics failed humankind. Only with magic were they able to reach the stars...*" before going on to explain how wizards and sorcerers, with the help of the Chinese Monkey God, were able to punch holes through demon-infested realms, then use those to travel to other worlds.

You can do anything.

What's stopping you?

About the Author

Blaze Ward writes science fiction in the Alexandria Station universe (Jessica Keller, The Science Officer, The Story Road, etc.) as well as several other science fiction universes, such as Star Dragon, the Dominion, and more. He also writes odd bits of high fantasy with swords and orcs. In addition, he is the Editor and Publisher of *Boundary Shock Quarterly Magazine*. You can find out more at his website www.blazeward.com, as well as Facebook, Goodreads, and other places.

Blaze's works are available as ebooks, paper, and audio, and can be found at a variety of online vendors. His newsletter comes out regularly, and you can also follow his blog on his website. He really enjoys interacting with fans, and looks forward to any and all questions—even ones about his books!

Never miss a release!
If you'd like to be notified of new releases, sign up for my newsletter.

http://www.blazeward.com/newsletter/

Buy More!
Did you know that you can buy directly from my website?

https://www.blazeward.com/shop/

Connect with Blaze!

Web: www.blazeward.com
Boundary Shock Quarterly (BSQ):

About Knotted Road Press

Knotted Road Press fiction specializes in dynamic writing set in mysterious, exotic locations.

Knotted Road Press non-fiction publishes autobiographies, business books, cookbooks, and how-to books with unique voices.

Knotted Road Press creates DRM-free ebooks as well as high-quality print books for readers around the world.

With authors in a variety of genres including literary, poetry, mystery, fantasy, and science fiction, Knotted Road Press has something for everyone.

Knotted Road Press
www.KnottedRoadPress.com

www.ingramcontent.com/pod-product-compliance
Lightning Source LLC
Chambersburg PA
CBHW071115030426
42336CB00013BA/2097